Passive Income—

Your Automatic Money

Making Machine

Ma ZhiQiang

Passive Income- Your Automatic Money Making Machine

Ma ZhiQiang

Copyright © 2019 by Ma ZhiQiang All rights reserved.

The author reserves all rights to this book. They do not allow anyone to copy or distribute any part of the book, electronic or mechanical, in any way or form. No one has the right to store the information in this document in the retrieval system without the appropriate written permission of the publisher or author, nor is it authorized to make copies, record copies, scan portions of this document, etc.

Disclaimer

All information in this book is for informational and educational purposes only. The author does not interpret any results from the use of this article in any way. While conscious and creative attempts have been made to ensure that all information provided herein is as accurate and useful as possible, the author is not legally liable for any damages resulting from accuracy and use/abuse of this information.

Table of Contents

PREFACE THE REASON FOR WRITING THIS BOOK iv

PART I WHAT IS THE REAL WORLD 1
- ARE YOU TIRED? 1
- INFLATION IS BY YOUR SIDE 2
- WORLD AGING TREND 4
- PASSIVE INCOME ESSENCE 6

PART II CREATE YOUR OWN AUTOMATIC MONEY MAKING MACHINE 8
- YOUTUBE VIDEO 8
- UNIQUE FORMS OF AMAZON FBA 12
- PASSIVE INCOME OF E-BOOKS 13
- REAL ESTATE PROJECTS 15
- UNEXPECTED FORMS OF PASSIVE INCOME 20

PART III BREAKING THE MIND, SEEING THE WORLD OF MONEY 23
- MISUNDERSTANDING OF PASSIVE INCOME RECOGNITION 23
- CREATE YOUR OWN PORTFOLIO OF INCOME MODEL 24

Preface

Undoubtedly, we are now in the era and wave of the Internet. In the face of the pressure of life, rising prices and rising inflation, in addition to traditional investment channels (stocks, real estate, funds, etc.), what can be done? Defending our money, passive income, financial freedom is an ideal state of life, everyone wants to own, through this book you can understand that through the Internet you can also easily achieve passive income and achieve financial freedom

PART I WHAT IS THE REAL WORLD

Are you tired?

Inflation is by your side

World aging trend

Passive income essence

ARE YOU TIRED?

When you go to work by bus, you will find out what is overcrowded; when you take the subway, you will understand the general principle of crowding; when driving, and you will feel the crowded traffic.... Every day we spend on commuting Time is already a lot, what are you doing in the busy and crowded days, are you tired?

Why are people always busy during their lifetime? That is because we are afraid. We are afraid of falling because we are afraid of no income. Once people stop working at hand, they would get annoyed. This is why people are especially uncomfortable when they are alone at night. Because when they stop everything, they will have extra time to think about their own life. Once they find that they are busy, they will feel scared when they have no other achievements. They are afraid that they will not leave anything when they reach the end.

Because you are using your precious time to exchange money. When your position or small business is running better, you will feel tired. You can't stop and you can only work hard. Like rich father, poor father Kiyosaki said that because you have no assets, there is no passive income. Buffett said that if you don't find a way to earn money when you sleep, you will always work to death! Some people 9 to 5 a day. I work 7 hours a day and then work hard to work overtime. I will not work more than 24 hours a day. This way the income for a day is limited and there is no income if you don't go to work. For your boss, you are the asset of your boss. Even if he sleeps at home, you create value for your boss like a machine. It is more important that you lose the opportunity and possibility of creating wealth only to ban your main things for the busy work. It is your brain because it has stopped turning. This book is mainly to share some specific methods and experiences of passive income for your reference. If you also like passive income or you want to build your own passive income and want to lie down to make money while you sleep. This book is very suitable for you. If you are an office worker and still work 9 to 5, looking for a part-time job, then the book will recommend several methods for you to use.

INFLATION IS BY YOUR SIDE

In 2019 and in the next few years, the whole of China will be in the process of "adjusting" the macroeconomic structure. In this process of "adjustment", the only constant will be the acceleration of M2 data. At the same time, the debt of the Ministry of Finance has increased simultaneously.

PASSIVE INCOME

Although the Ministry of Finance announced that the overall local debt size in January 2019 was 1,880.41 million Yuan, the local financing platform and hidden debt did not provide more multidimensional data, the specific situation is exactly what it is.

Macroeconomic M1, M2 statistics from 2018 to 2019.

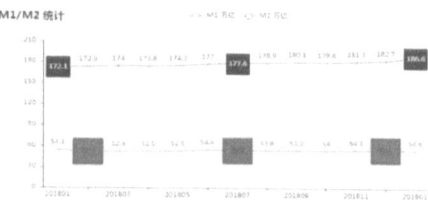

In a brief explanation, the above figure is the M1 and M2 data from last year to this year. It is very clear that the M1 data remained basically unchanged from January 2018 to January this year, while the M2 data increased from 172 trillion to 186.6 trillion. Simply speaking, M2 has expanded by at least 186.6/172*100% ~%10 in the absence of significant changes in household deposits and corporate deposits.

In other words, as long as you hold the Renminbi at least the hard currency, inflation loss is around 10%. Inflation is eroding your purse a little bit every year. Do you feel it?

PASSIVE INCOME

WORLD AGING TREND

Population issues are one of the most important social problems in the world and the core of many contemporary social problems. According to UN statistics, by 2050, the world population will reach 9-10 billion, of which the population over 60 will reach 2 billion. The population over 65 will reach 1.5 billion by 2050, and will soon exceed the number of children under 5 years old. On the other hand, with the advancement of science and technology and the improvement of medical standards, the life expectancy of the world's population has been prolonged. Under such circumstances, many people must re-plan their retirement plans, or postpone retirement, or even retire, in order to maintain stable income. Controlling population growth is imminent, and the issue of aging is the most prominent problem in population issues.

In recent years, European countries have successively reformed their retirement systems and gradually extended their retirement age. The reform of the retirement system is mainly due to the aggravation of the global population aging and the low fertility rate in some countries and the fact that pensions exceed the budget. The retirement age in developed countries is generally higher than 65 years old!

Germany over the next few decades or raise the retirement age to 69 years, in order to ensure the basic operation of the retirement system, the German government has taken a number of reform measures. Among them, the most important measure is to delay the retirement age to 67 years no later than 2029. If you have to retire early because of health and other reasons, you can only get part of the pension; only after reaching the retirement age can you get the full amount. The German government emphasizes that the existing plans to postpone the retirement age are sufficient to cover the cost of Germany's increasingly aging population.

Japan is everywhere to see the hard work of the elderly in their 60s. According to the calculations of the National Institute of Social Security and Population Research of Japan, the aging population in Japan will account for 30% of the total population in 2024 and will rise to 40.5% in 2055. Aging population poses two main problems, one large pension gap; Second, many elderly people lead to high medical costs, social security costs in Japan each year at a rate of 1 trillion yen in growth.

Iceland, although the Icelandic government stipulates that the age of pensions for the elderly is 67, in Iceland, the retirement age for men is 70 and for women 65.

The retirement age in Italy is 62 years old. Italy adopted a flexible delayed retirement age policy in 1995 and 2004. Mainly to raise the retirement age by increasing the pension payment period: In 1995, the policy requires that if the insured person has paid the fee for 35 years, he or she can choose to retire at any age between the ages of 57 and 65. The validity period is 2035. In 2004, it was proposed that male employees should have two conditions at the same time: the pension insurance has been paid for 35 years and reached the minimum age standard (the minimum age standard for 2008 is 60 years old, 2010 is 61 years old, and 2014 is 62 years old).

Australia's retirement age: 65 years and a half, Australians are currently 65 years old, starting from July 1, 2017, starting to change to 65 and a half, and then increase by half a year. In 2014, the Australian Treasury Department recommended that the retirement age be postponed to 70 years from 2053.

PASSIVE INCOME ESSENCE

Bank financial planners usually recommend us to buy wealth management products, bank deposits, etc. However, the annualized rate of return of such wealth management products is simply not enough to resist inflation. It does not have the effect of resisting inflation. Instead, it will sink deeper and deeper in the quagmire. What should we do in the face of the dual pressures of inflation and population aging? Active income is the income that we actively obtain. We pay mental or physical labor through work, and exchange money, such as wage income, with time, physical strength, energy, and wisdom. Passive income means that we don't need to

PASSIVE INCOME

spend too much time and energy, but we can earn income through proper investment or financial management. Such as the rent of the house, the dividends of the stock, the copyright fees of the writer, and so on. In turn, the real rich, 90% of the family income structure is passive income, they have a lot of time to freely control, can accompany their families, travel, do what they like to do. They don't have to worry about money because they have a constant passive income to meet the needs of everyday life. Therefore, we need to constantly adjust our income structure so that passive income becomes our main source of income, in order to reduce the anxiety of life and to obtain a happy life. There is no income after sleep, life is half-way, don't dare to get sick, don't dare to get sick, don't dare to die, how sad is it?

PART II CREATE YOUR OWN AUTOMATIC MONEY MAKING MACHINE

YouTube video

The unique form of Amazon's FBA

Passive income of e-books

Real estate projects

Unexpected form of passive income

Now is the age of the Internet, In addition to traditional founding companies and investing in real estate. If you don't have big money or if you are a student, as long as you have a computer and a mobile phone, you can still create your own passive income system. The premise is to spend your time and energy. Creating passive income cannot be done overnight. It can't be done in a few days. Before this, you need to have a psychological standard ready, but with the manifestation of cumulative benefits, once the project is on the right track, you will find it easier to make money later.

YOUTUBE VIDEO

YouTube is the second largest website on the Internet and the largest video site in the world. It has billions of page views every day. Such huge traffic will naturally generate opportunities to make money. Now more and more people are there. Making money by uploading videos on YouTube, the most powerful broadcasters have earned more than a few million dollars on YouTube. It can be said that it is entirely possible to eat and drink by taking video and to embark on the peak of life. Of course, first of all, first you have to be able to shoot a very powerful video. If you don't have the ability, you can't make money. Of course, it's not. As the saying goes, there is traffic that can be realized naturally even if you can't shoot it that much good. You don't have to worry about making powerful videos. There are still many ways to make money through YouTube. Here are six ways to make money.

1. This is One of the Best Ways to Make Money on YouTube
Most broadcasters earn the first bucket of gold through an official partnership program. The YouTube partnership program allows video creators to make money by displaying ads in the video. YouTube calculates the specific amount of profit based on the number of times the ad is displayed. So when you have a lot of people watching your videos, you can make a lot of money. As long as your video is good enough, you can naturally make a profit. But when you are lucky, like the famous Charlie bites my finger. A short film of less than a minute, with more than 800 million page views, the broadcaster directly received more than 4 million dividends, which is really awkward, because it is the largest video site in the world with the huge traffic, and you don't know why, for a sudden, there is a video bursting red, and then it becomes a viral video, which spreads all over the world, even if it is boring, you can get a high page view, then it is really lying. Make money.

PASSIVE INCOME

2. Make Money Through Fan Sponsorship

The above method is done by hanging advertisements officially that is directly divided with you. Although it is convenient, if the video doesn't have a good page view, the income is very small. So, we can also make money directly through fan sponsorship. As long as your video is liked, you can directly reward you, but the temporary sponsorship function is only valid in the following regions: Australia, France, Mexico, Spain, the United Kingdom, the United States, and Japan.

3. Sell Goods Directly Through Your Channel

If your video has a suitable theme, you can also sell the goods directly. In this way, when viewers watch your video, if they like the product, they can purchase it directly. For example, your video is about clothing matching, you can sell clothes directly. After the channel has certain fans, you can also customize the T-shirt for sale, so you can earn more money. The most important thing is that you don't need to join the cooperation plan, there are no restrictions.

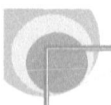

4. Make Money Through Affiliate Marketing

If you don't have a product channel or if you feel that your sales are too much terrible, you can also promote their products directly through alliances such as Amazon and earn sales commissions. Although you don't have the money to sell your own products, you can save time and effort, and don't have to worry about shipping.

5. Link Location on the Sales Video

YouTube is the world's largest video site. The function is very powerful, video HD and with powerful analysis management tools. You can translate subtitles directly and add external links to your videos. Because YouTube can add external links to the video, point links to other YouTube videos, channels, playlists, and external websites. So you can post the sale information directly. If someone wants you to help promote his channel or video, you can contact him to add his channel or video link to your video by paying for it, but this may require good negotiation skills. The better you talk, the higher would be your income.

6. Drain to Your Own Website

It's a great way to make money by directing videos to your own website and then making money by advertising on your own website. You can also do other CPA alliances to make money.

PASSIVE INCOME

UNIQUE FORMS OF AMAZON FBA

Amazon (FBA), Amazon distribution mode, Amazon warehousing delivery. It is to stock the goods to the overseas Amazon warehouse in advance. After the store orders, there is a warehouse on the Amazon site that is directly delivered to the customer's hand. The operation of Jingdong's warehouse is basically the same. The time is fast, and the customer experience is high. The world's e-commerce trade is growing rapidly, and it is difficult to stand out from the competition. If you spend a lot of time picking up, packing, shipping, and shopping..., then do you still have time to promote and improve your product? Do you still have time to expand the market? Many sellers find that when they are responsible for order processing and delivery. Manual processing fees, warehouse maintenance costs, and system upgrade costs will account for a large portion of the profit. Many seller's products will experience the peak season of sales spikes and the intermittent weak season. But the warehouse rent and the commission of the order operator, these fixed costs, are always the same. As an Amazon seller, if you want to reduce costs and speed up delivery, the most effective measure is to have an overseas warehouse. To help you with logistics, you only need to send the goods to the overseas warehouse in batches and process the delivery order online. Then the Internet will replace a series of complicated logistics processes such as picking up goods, comparing, packing, ordering, and shipping.

Advantages of FBA:

1. Improve the ranking of listings, help sellers become featured sellers, grab shopping carts, increase customer trust, and increase sales.
2. Years of rich logistics experience, warehouses all over the world, intelligent management.
3. Delivery time is super-fast (most warehouses are close to the airport)

4. 24/7 Amazon professional customer service, no need to worry about customer service, save a lot of labor costs.
5. Erasing bad disputes caused by logistics.

The Difference Between Amazon and Domestic E-commerce

The operating focus is different from Amazon's operations. All of them know that Amazon pays attention to products that are more important than shops. This is a different reason for the domestic Ali series e-commerce platform. The A9 station search engine algorithm gives you free traffic. You only need excellent products, no matter who you are. You can get good sales on the Amazon platform. In China, we sell our products through various methods such as through train and improve the visibility of the store through various means. Because domestic people have a habit of shopping, they click on the sales ranking list. The platform of heavy products and light stores is also very important for the products and despise shops, but the products you choose must also be good. This requires you to have unique selection of techniques and selection methods. Amazon's unique logistics and customer service advantages have greatly reduced labor costs and capital costs, allowing merchants to shift their focus to merchandise and greatly reduce the burden on merchants so that businesses can have time to create the best products.

PASSIVE INCOME OF E-BOOKS

In 2010, the famous futurist and author of Digital Survival, Negroponte, predicted that the emergence of e-books in five years would completely replace paper books. Although this prophecy was not implemented on the

Kindle, it does not deny the epoch-making significance of the Kindle to the paper book market and the publishing industry.

Amazon China's survey found that the current proportion of users reading both paper and electronic versions are increasing. Different from popular cognition, paper and e-books carry the relationship between data and paper. It shows that the relationship between paper books and e-books is actually mutually reinforcing. The simultaneous distribution of paper books and e-books is becoming an industry trend.

According to the data of Amazon China, the ratio of the simultaneous release of the book and the electronic version of the book in 2017 increased by nearly 60% compared with 2016, and the sales of the paper and electronic version of the simultaneous book in 2017 were the same as the non-paper synchronization book. More than one. In addition, the data shows that Kindle e-book readers have sold millions of units in China. China has become the largest market for Amazon's global Kindle device sales since the end of 2016. As of now, the total number of books in the Kindle China e-bookstore is nearly 700,000. It is nearly 10 times more than in 2013. In addition, the readers' willingness to pay for reading is significantly enhanced. In 2017, the number of downloads of Kindle paid e-books and the number of Kindle paying users increased by 10 times and 12 times respectively compared with 2013.

With the continued popularity of digital reading, more and more audiences are reading e-books. Twenty-three percent of respondents said they mainly read e-books in the past year, a 4% increase over 2018. The survey also showed that e-reading played a good role in the total reading, with 71% of respondents indicating an increase in their total reading after they started reading e-books. If you have good ideas and writing talent, it is a good choice to put books on the Amazon platform. Maybe you will say that you can't write. You can also find a professional writer to do it for you. As long as you say your own thoughts, they will help you with everything. It is very simple. At the end of the book, there is a freelance website. You can find relevant information on it.

REAL ESTATE PROJECTS

In the past few decades, the real estate industry has been in a very prosperous stage. Inflation has intensified, and the rapid appreciation of paper money has rapidly appreciated. Especially for those who invest in real estate and get rich. They are immersed in the joy of fighting victory. I don't want to learn other ways of managing money. There are several drawbacks in investing in real estate today.

1. The return on investment is very low
2. Transaction cost tax is very high
3. National regulatory policies.

The emphasis here is that I am not saying that do not invest in real estate. Just too low return on investment will increase its investment risk and control ability. It has many indicators to control the analysis but the only important indicator is the monthly positive cash flow. Once the cash flow is positive and larger the value, the better the risk can be avoided. An important indicator of investment in property is cash flow, not capital gains (sales and sales of real estate). Some people only pay attention to housing prices, just like paying attention to stock prices. This simple expectation is only a profit model that makes money in a rising cycle, but the essence is gambling. In the age of inflation, rents generally rose. The monthly repayment of bank loans remains the same, and rents rise due to inflation, so this creates more cash flow.

Here are a few examples of how to improve your return on investment.

1. Global Asset Allocation, Look to the World
Now, if you still think that the center of overseas investment is in Europe and America, and that "Cambodia is the biggest poor village in the world", then you are once again deceived by your own stereotypes. There will always be people who look at China in the 1990s. The view looks at countries that are more backward than us. But this stereotype does exist because, before 2012, most wealthy households in China concentrated their overseas real estate investments in developed countries such as the United States, Australia, Canada, the United Kingdom, and Europe. In recent years, more and more people have begun to turn to Southeast Asia, such as Thailand, Malaysia, and the Philippines.

Moreover, many well-known domestic enterprises have also entered Southeast Asian countries. For the whole of Southeast Asia, there are not many countries with investment value. Cambodia is one of them.

PASSIVE INCOME

According to data released by the Ministry of Land Planning and Construction of Cambodia, the investment in the construction industry in Cambodia in the first four months of this year reached 2.742 billion US dollars, an increase of 67% compared with the same period in 2018. This also shows that the real estate industry in Cambodia is growing steadily, and a large number of high-end apartments and Office building projects have blossomed, and more and more investment options are available.

As we all know, the investment return rate in Cambodia is far ahead of other countries in Southeast Asia. According to Hurun Research Institute's latest "2018 Annual Overseas Investment Return Index", Phnom Penh has a return on investment of 29.4% and 6.5%. The rental return rate ranks first and fourth in the world, respectively, and steady cash flow income.

Ranking	Ranking changes	City	2018 Annual return on investment (A+B+C)	2017 Annual return on investment	Annual rise in house prices	B Rate of Return on Rent	Change of Exchange Rate of Local Currency to RMB	Country

YOUR AUTOMATIC MONEY MAKING MACHINE

1	Newly added	PHNOM PENH	29.4%	/	16.7%	6.5%	6.2%	Cambodia
2	↑33	Las Vegas	23.9%	12.4%	12.8%	5.3%	5.7%	U.S.A
3	↑13	San Jose	23.8%	17.3%	13%	5.1%	5.7%	U.S.A
4	↑19	Nashville	20.8%	14.7%	9%	6%	5.7%	U.S.A
5	↑35	Rolando	20.7%	10.5%	9.3%	5.7%	5.7%	U.S.A
6	Newly added	Philadelphia	20.5%	/	11.8%	3%	5.7%	U.S.A
7	↑16	Hong Kong	20.3%	14.7	13.3%	1.6%	5.4%	china
8	↑40	Houston	19.8%	8.7%	6.9%	7.2%	5.7%	U.S.A
9	↑20	Osaka	19%	13.1%	7.7%	2.8%	8.5%	Japan
10	Newly added	Phoenix	18.9%	/	7.7%	5.5%	5.7%	U.S.A

2. B&B Bed and Breakfast, Airbnb

B&B is a kind of accommodation products that are very dependent on tourism resources, and are mostly distributed in popular tourist destinations in China. Statistics show that the transaction volume of China's online accommodation market in 2013 reached 41.21 billion yuan. In 2016, the transaction scale of China's online accommodation market exceeded 100 billion yuan. As of 2017, the transaction volume of China's online accommodation market increased to 158.62 billion yuan, a year on year increase of 26.8%.

After the decoration of the house or the rented house, the housekeeper and the cleaning will be arranged to let it operate on its own, and it can effectively play its role and form a system of automatic management. Or directly to the platform, the model of income 3 and 7 is also a form of passive income.

In China, each city is slightly different. The price of a short-term rental house is 1.5-2 times that of a long-term rental house. It has a larger income than a long-term rental house and can bring positive cash flow to the greatest extent. In the era of inflation, with the depreciation of banknotes, the price of the hotel will rise, the turnover and profits will rise. If it is your own house, after the renovation, do the homestay, and the monthly bank loan will remain unchanged. As the price of the home is rising, the income will be even greater. If it is a rented house, you can use the long-term lease method of 5-10 years to keep the fixed cost unchanged, thus expanding the benefits.

3. REITs

If you ask if there is a simple way to invest in real estate and have a good return on investment, then it should be REITs. Real estate investment trusts (REITs) is a securitization of real estate important tool. Real estate securitization is a financial transaction process that converts low-liquidity, non-securities real estate investment directly into securities assets in the capital market. Real estate securitization includes two basic forms of real estate project financing securitization and real estate mortgage loan securitization. The characteristics of EITs are as follows:

1. Revenue mainly comes from rental income and real estate appreciation;
2. Most of the proceeds will be used to distribute dividends;

REITs have higher long-term returns. The charm of REITs lies in: through the "collection" of funds, it provides opportunities for small and medium investors to invest in lucrative real estate industry; professional managers use the funds raised for real estate investment portfolios to diversify real estate investment risks; the equity owned by the person can be transferred and has good liquidity. Analysis of current interest rate trends, if the global rate of return is 6% -8% real estate investment trust REITs, should be a very good choice.

Of course, the methods to increase the return on real estate investment are not limited to the above. Buying a house for rectification, changing the room to two rooms, buying a house in the court, buying a house on the first floor, changing the house, buying a dilapidated house and a house with various problems for decoration and rental, long-term renting Splitting rentals, homestays in the United States, and renting out in Taiwan can all increase the return on investment.

UNEXPECTED FORMS OF PASSIVE INCOME

Into the supermarket, the shelves of pet cats, pets and dogs dedicated goods more and more, dazzling, it seems that overnight, the city's major shopping malls and supermarkets have set up a pet supplies area, the pet trading market is also booming. According to statistics, the annual transaction volume of Chinese pets and supplies has exceeded 10 billion Yuan. Not only that, but a complete industrial chain behind the pet has gradually formed: pet farms, pet hospitals, pet grooming shops, pet food stores, pet foster stores, pet tombs, and even pet websites, which not only form a rather large The market has also created a new term: the pet economy.

PASSIVE INCOME

In the age of the Internet, there will be more opportunities, more imaginable opportunities, if your vision is limited to assets, such as real estate stocks and other traditional investment products. Prove that you have been abandoned by the current era. Because your assets can also be pets at all. In the tourist scenic area, when the peak season is reached, the tourists are in a constant stream. The profit of riding a camel can range from tens of Yuan to 100 Yuan, only a few dozen minutes. A day's profit can be easily more than a few thousand RMB。

PASSIVE INCOME

There is a businessman in Hong Kong. He has a ranch in Australia. He specializes in raising high-quality horses. Most of the horses he raises are stallions. They do not count the other income generated by horses. They are only breeding and borrowing. Give him a steady stream of cash every month.

In addition, passive income can also be the advertising revenue of the website, the copyright of the published songs, the copyright of the movie, uploading of photos to a website, the automatic car washing machine, the company that operates automatically, the stock of high dividends are the forms of passive income. Everything can be an asset or a debt. The key is to use their people to improve their financial quotient to constantly train and learn to build their own passive income system and to find a golden goose that can give you a golden egg.

PART III BREAKING THE MIND, SEEING THE WORLD OF MONEY

Misunderstanding of passive income recognition

Create your own portfolio of income model

Financial quotient needs to exercise and keep learning. When you master the laws of money, you will see a world of money. If you want to buy an Apple phone, how would you buy it? Of course, most people will choose to go directly to buy, of course, it is ok, but it is not the best choice, because the money you spend will take up your cash flow, without any meaning. Those who have been trained in financial business will carry out the longest period and will have a small monthly fee. Then they will invest the other products in the investment, and the proceeds will cover the cost of the installment. There are many similar examples. If you buy a car for your own use, the monthly parking fee, fuel fee, maintenance fee, etc., are all your liabilities. If the car you buy is paid in installments and then used for wedding leasing, the monthly cash flow income will cover the debt and there will be positive cash flow. So good at using other people's money, other people's time, make good use of leverage, build your assets, it is the smart choice. When you find an opportunity and put it into practice, let you earn the first bucket of gold, your thinking will get opened because you have found a world of money, you will find the next second chance to make money, the first three opportunities to make money and so on.

MISUNDERSTANDING OF PASSIVE INCOME RECOGNITION

Everyone on the Internet from the media video platform or posts often see some exaggerated headlines into hundreds of dollars into the title of thousands of dollars per month. But the real thing is not like this. These people who send this information are outdated and most people have heard that the reason they write this title is to use everyone's traffic and traffic to make money, this is their purpose.

Affiliate marketing/ Shopify / Amazon FBA and so on have no problems, but in the early stage, you have to spend a lot of time and energy. They are unlikely to make you rich overnight. You need to constantly research this project, keep practicing, and constantly Make mistakes, keep correcting, and they may be far more difficult than you think, and some passive income is not something you can do completely, just don't need time to exchange money. The characteristics of these projects are that once the project is on the right track, there will be a snowball effect. The area of the snowball is very small at first, but you will continue to push it. The area where the snowball sticks will become larger, so that it can effect passively.

CREATE YOUR OWN PORTFOLIO OF INCOME MODEL

Use the time to exchange assets, instead of taking time to exchange money, and then let the acquired assets work for you. It can continue to work and you use passive income to exchange time to create assets and then generate cash flow from these assets. In order to make the snowballs roll more when the passive income is greater than the active income, the financial freedom is realized.

PASSIVE INCOME

If you only have one type of passive income, then this form of income is a bit singular. If this problem occurs, it will directly affect your income and living standards. Therefore, to create a multi-channel diversified passive income, to build your own aircraft carrier, in order to be invincible, in order to more effectively resist the risk. In passive income, the passive income type is also subdivided, and the low return rate is stably classified as defensive, and some high-yield products, but unstable, are classified as offensive.

For example, defensive types such as rented homestays are relatively stable and long-term benefits. If you want your aircraft carrier to drive faster, you can also configure some radical passive income, such as online stores, FBA or high-dividend stocks. The result is high returns, but there will be volatility and uncertainty. This combination will balance the two and keep the overall rate of return stable. Hong Kong businessman starman, the combination of financing leverage and bond+retis, receives up to 6 digits of passive income per month.

There are many such programs and models. You can design your own arrangements according to your own hobbies but you can't copy other people's models. The method you think of is the best for you. If you can't get out of work now, or if you are a student who needs to work part-time, here are a few websites that can help you.

https://www.fiverr.com Freelance website

https://www.upwork.com/ Freelance website

PASSIVE INCOME

https://www.wyzant.com/ A website that teaches language to make money

https://cn.dreamstime.com/ Upload photos to make money on the site

https://teespring.com Design a T-shirt to make money on the website

https://www.squadhelp.com/ the website that makes money

https://www.gmrtranscription.com/ A transcription website that makes money

https://www.rev.com/ make money through transcribing

This book is just to share some experiences, broaden your horizons and open up your thinking. Passive income can be light asset online stores, short videos, e-books, heavy-asset real estate, or interesting pets. The key is how to find a way to passive income, and create your own money-making system. This book is not a reference book and a tutorial. It can't be a hard copy. It's just a book that shares your experience. Finally, I hope that everyone can gain financial freedom through their own efforts. I hope this book will help and enlighten everyone. If you like this book, you are welcome to forward the major websites and communities to reward the author's hard work.

If you have any questions, please feel free to communicate in the following ways.

Author Email:cashf6651@gmail.com

QQ:276415010@qq.com

PASSIVE INCOME

www.ingramcontent.com/pod-product-compliance
Lightning Source LLC
Chambersburg PA
CBHW021854170526
45157CB00006B/2446